P9-DDC-689

To:
From:
Date:

ZONDERVAN

The Weekly Self-Care Project

© 2021 Zondervan

Requests for information should be addressed to:
Zondervan, *3900 Sparks Dr. SE, Grand Rapids, Michigan 49546*

ISBN 978-0-310-46016-9 (hardcover)

Unless otherwise noted, Scripture quotations are taken from the Holy Bible, New International Version®, NIV®. Copyright © 1973, 1978, 1984, 2011 by Biblica, Inc.® Used by permission of Zondervan. All rights reserved worldwide. www.zondervan.com. The "NIV" and "New International Version" are trademarks registered in the United States Patent and Trademark Office by Biblica, Inc.®

Scripture quotations marked ESV are taken from the ESV® Bible (The Holy Bible, English Standard Version®). Copyright © 2001 by Crossway, a publishing ministry of Good News Publishers. Used by permission. All rights reserved.

Scripture quotations marked GNT are taken from the Good New Translation in Today's English Version—Second Edition. Copyright © 1992 by American Bible Society. Used by permission.

Scripture quotations marked THE MESSAGE are taken from THE MESSAGE. Copyright © 1993, 2002, 2018 by Eugene H. Peterson. Used by permission of NavPress. All rights reserved. Represented by Tyndale House Publishers, a Division of Tyndale House Ministries.

Scripture quotations marked NKJVare taken from the New King James Version®. Copyright © 1982 by Thomas Nelson. Used by permission. All rights reserved.

Scripture quotations marked NLT are taken from the Holy Bible, New Living Translation. Copyright © 1996, 2004, 2015 by Tyndale House Foundation. Used by permission of Tyndale House Ministries, Carol Stream, Illinois 60188. All rights reserved.

Scripture quotations marked THE VOICE are taken from The Voice™. Copyright © 2012 by Ecclesia Bible Society. Used by permission. All rights reserved. Note: Italics in quotations from The Voice are used to "indicate words not directly tied to the dynamic translation of the original language" but that "bring out the nuance of the original, assist in completing ideas, and . . . provide readers with information that would have been obvious to the original audience" (The Voice, preface).

Any internet addresses (websites, blogs, etc.) and telephone numbers in this book are offered as a resource. They are not intended in any way to be or imply an endorsement by Zondervan, nor does Zondervan vouch for the content of these sites and numbers for the life of this book.

All rights reserved. No part of this publication may be reproduced, stored in a retrieval system, or transmitted in any form or by any means—electronic, mechanical, photocopy, recording, or any other—except for brief quotations in printed reviews, without the prior permission of the publisher.

Art direction and cover design: Tiffany Forrester
Cover and interior photography: Noelle Glaze
Interior design: Emily Ghattas

Printed in China

21 22 23 24 25 GRI 10 9 8 7 6 5 4 3 2 1

THE WEEKLY SELF-CARE PROJECT

A CHALLENGE TO JOURNAL, REFLECT, AND INVITE BALANCE

Contents

Emotional Care

Mental Care

How to Use This Journal

"Love your neighbor as yourself."

MATTHEW 22:39 NKJV

Jesus commanded each of us to love our neighbors *as ourselves.* He charged us with loving others the *same way we love ourselves.* Think about how you treat yourself, how you speak about yourself. Would you treat the people around you in the same way? Would you push them to stay up late to get a little more done, to skip meals to fit in one more meeting, or to squash their emotions because they're inconvenient? The reality is that we're often far kinder to those around us than we are to ourselves.

We can't pour from an empty cup. If you aren't treating yourself the way you would care for those dearest to you, then this book is for you. It's a tool to help you intentionally, biblically, and tenderly care for yourself—body, mind, heart, and soul—so that you have the energy and resources to go out into this world and share God's love with others.

Each week invites you to read from the Bible and then respond to journaling prompts and calls to action. These cues, modeled in Scripture, will challenge you to rethink how to care for yourself and how you see yourself. Start at the beginning or jump ahead to the section that calls out to you.

Self-care isn't only about indulging in momentary pleasures. It's about taking action to help yourself become whole, healthy, and able to serve God from a place of joy and abundance. This year, be intentional in how you care for yourself, and watch how it deepens and strengthens your connection with your Creator, the One who always treats you with love and tender care.

Physical Care

Be Filled with Good

They all depend on you to give them food as they need it. When you supply it, they gather it. You open your hand to feed them, and they are richly satisfied.

PSALM 104:27–28 NLT

Different words for *rest* are found more than 250 times in the Bible. In the Old Testament, we see the Hebrew words *nuach,* which means "to rest or to be quiet," and *shabat*, which means "to cease or to rest." In the New Testament, we find the Greek word *anapausis,* which means "cessation or refreshment." Rest, quiet, and refreshment. These words give us a picture of how God wants us to understand rest.

If we're being honest, most of us don't see much rest, quiet, cessation, or refreshment in our everyday lives. Even when you think you're relaxing—watching TV, reading, or scrolling through social media or the news—you aren't being refreshed. Most of us are always busy, living in a near-constant state of stress and feeling overwhelmed. But that's not the plan God has for you. He desires you to do His work, work that allows margin for refreshment in His peace and stability. He calls you to rest so you can be restored and strengthened. When you cease striving and stop clinging to the busyness of life, you open up space in your mind and heart that God will fill. And when your body and mind are restored and rested, He will fill you with His goodness, which gives you the strength, courage, and hope to continue doing the work He has called you to.

WEEK 1

Treat Yourself Well

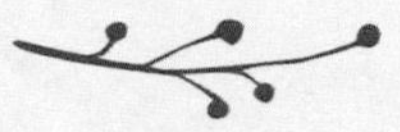

Therefore honor God with your bodies.

1 CORINTHIANS 6:20

We've all seen how self-care is pictured on TV and in movies: bubble baths, shopping, fancy wine and chocolate, and nights out. But true self-care isn't only about treating yourself—it's about treating yourself well. It's about identifying your needs and addressing them.

The easiest place to start is by taking a look at how you care for your body. When you honor your body, you position yourself to be a force for good, to love those around you. Are you treating it like a temple? Or a crumbling shack?

In the space below, write down the ways you already care for your body each week.

Where do you see room for improvement?

WEEK 2

Back to Basics

Then, because so many people were coming and going that they did not even have a chance to eat, he said to them, "Come with me by yourselves to a quiet place and get some rest."

MARK 6:31

Needs are called that for a reason; they are what your body *needs* to function. They are not optional. Jesus knew that and urged His disciples to eat and drink, to rest and have quiet time. If it was important to Jesus, doesn't it make sense that caring for your body should be important to you? To keep your body healthy, you need adequate sleep, nutritious meals, plenty of water, opportunities to move and stretch, and quiet time to restore your equilibrium.

What does your body need today?

Which of your needs are you most guilty of ignoring?

Are there new routines you can put into place to help address those needs? Write down your ideas.

WEEK 3

Clean It Up

She watches over the affairs of her household
and does not eat the bread of idleness.

PROVERBS 31:27

Cleaning is an act of self-care that isn't discussed often, but it's a powerful one. It's an instant boost to your spirits to take a long, hot bath and then climb into a freshly made bed with crisp, clean sheets or to walk into a tidy home with everything put away in its place. A sink piled high with dishes, a scummy shower, or surfaces piled with clutter can make your mind feel just as cluttered and murky. Roll up your sleeves and clean up your spaces for an instant feeling of refreshment.

How do you feel when everything is clean versus when your home or spaces are messy?

Plan a weekly or monthly cleaning schedule to help you stay on top of keeping things tidy.

WEEK 4

Get a System

A person without self-control is like a city with broken-down walls.

PROVERBS 25:28 NLT

Cleaning and organizing go hand in hand. It's far easier to keep things clean when all of your items have a designated spot. Get organized. It will take self-control to get into the habit, but living in a constant state of mess and chaos is not caring for yourself well. Get rid of or donate extra stuff, find a home for everything you own, and do a quick tidy up every day. Even small acts of organizing will compound through the days and weeks and keep you on a system for success. Being able to find what you need when you need it will make your life easier and less stressful.

Do you consider yourself to be organized? Why or why not?

Which room or space should you start with to get your stuff under control?

Write down a plan to get your home organized and stick with it. Your future self will thank you!

WEEK 5

Plan Ahead

For we are God's handiwork, created in Christ Jesus to do good works, which God prepared in advance for us to do.

EPHESIANS 2:10

Plan out your days (as best you can) to make room to care for your body with healthy meals, exercise, and plenty of sleep. Set a bedtime, and turn out the lights promptly each night. Create a meal plan each week (Taco Tuesday, anyone?), and put the trip to the grocery store on your calendar. Make plans for doctor appointments, dentist trips, and other routine care well in advance so you don't forget. These are commitments you are making to yourself and should be prioritized and treated as important as anything else on the calendar.

What are your favorite nutritious meals to make for yourself?

How much sleep do you need each night to feel your best?

When was the last time you had a physical or a routine dental cleaning? Do you need to schedule one? If yes, make it a priority to get an appointment on your schedule.

WEEK 6

You Are God's Temple

Do you not know that you are the temple of God and that the Spirit of God dwells in you?

1 CORINTHIANS 3:16 NKJV

The Spirit of God dwells in you. Maybe you don't always feel as though you deserve to be treated well, but knowing that something as beautiful, wonderful, and powerful as the Holy Spirit is part of you is a compelling reason to care for your body. One of the biggest stumbling blocks to finding a rhythm of self-care is an underlying belief that you aren't worthy of such love and tenderness from yourself. Have you found yourself looking inward and only seeing all the ways you don't measure up? God looks at you and sees His child, deserving of love and grace and all good things. He *chooses* to dwell in you, and that is abundant evidence that you are worthy and adored just as you are. Care for His temple—your body—with that in mind.

Why do you sometimes feel unworthy of self-care?

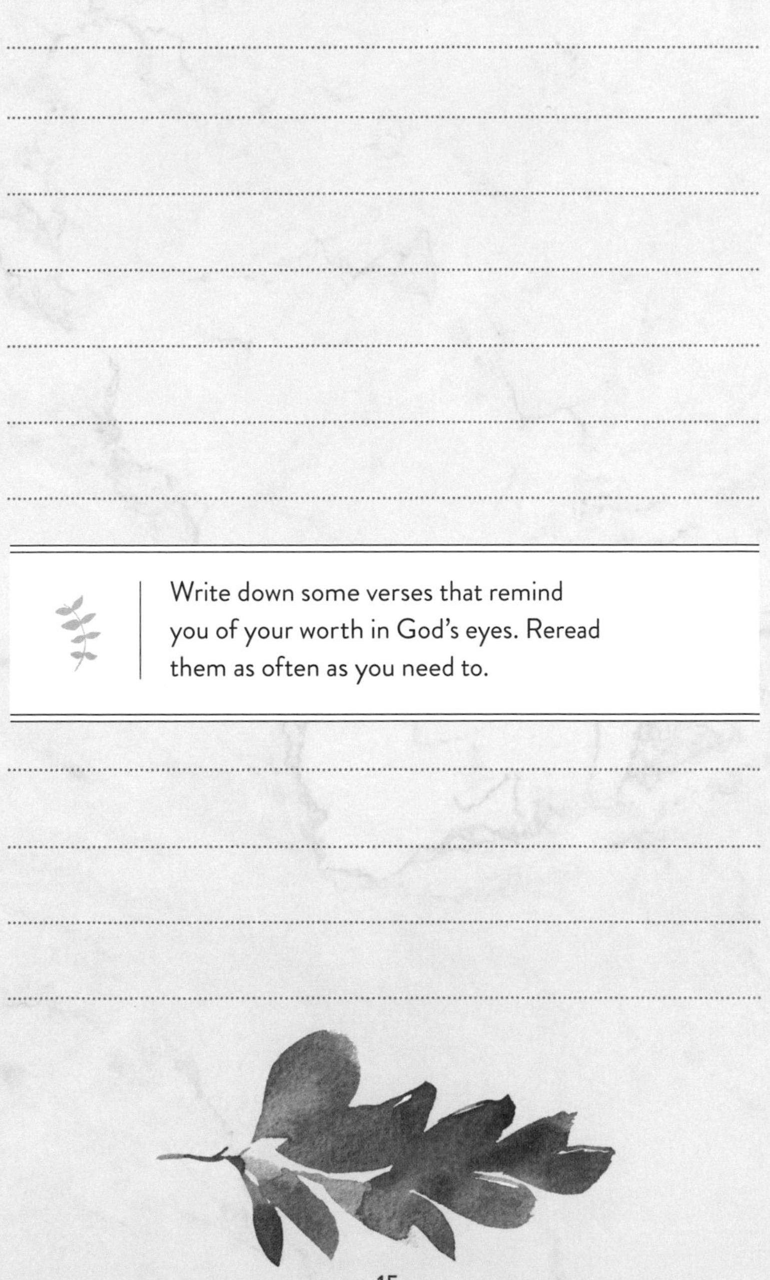

How does focusing on God's deep and unconditional love for you help you feel more deserving of love from yourself?

Write down some verses that remind you of your worth in God's eyes. Reread them as often as you need to.

WEEK 7

Overindulgence

Don't drink wine excessively. The drunken path is a reckless path. It leads nowhere. Instead, let God fill you with the Holy Spirit.

EPHESIANS 5:18 THE VOICE

A lot of times indulgence is confused for self-care. When you're stressed, the occasional glass of wine with dinner can easily become a nightly fixture. Or maybe you find yourself eating fast food or too much cake to avoid your feelings or even to cover up your feelings. Anything done in excess can become a dangerous dependence, especially if it's used in an unhealthy way. This behavior harms your body and is not the way to care for it. Don't mistake overindulgence for self-care. See it for what it is: excessive. Moderation is the path to self-care that God has laid out for us when it comes to treats and indulgences.

Is there anything you have been overindulging in lately?

What do you find yourself reaching for automatically when you get stressed, upset, or angry? Is it good for your body?

WEEK 8

Be Kind to Yourself

Don't let even one rotten word seep out of your mouths. Instead, offer only fresh words that build others up when they need it most. That way your good words will communicate grace to those who hear them.

EPHESIANS 4:29 THE VOICE

The words we use matter, both to ourselves and to others. The way you speak to yourself directly affects how you see yourself and how you treat yourself. When you speak kindly to yourself, you are more likely to see and treat yourself in loving ways. Your self-worth increases, and your desire to take care of yourself grows.

God created you with love and for His purpose. You are worthy of love, kindness, and care. Start your day today by looking in the mirror and telling your reflection:

- I am loved.
- I am valued.
- I am worthy.

You are not being arrogant or self-serving. You are speaking the truth of what God Himself has said about you. You are caring for yourself with the kindness and truth you are speaking. Practice this every day, starting with a week, and see how it changes your attitude, behavior, and feeling of self-worth.

What are other phrases or affirmations you can say to and about yourself?

WEEK 9

Take a Break

On the seventh day—with the canvas of the cosmos completed—God paused from His labor and rested. Thus God blessed day seven and made it special—an open time for pause and restoration, a sacred zone of Sabbath-keeping, because God rested from all the work He had done in creation that day.

GENESIS 2:2–3 THE VOICE

Sacred pause and restoration—doesn't that sound wonderful? Rest is more than sleep; it's also the time you take to do things that restore your energy and your relationship with your heavenly Father. Although every body needs something a little different, the average amount of sleep most people need every night is eight hours. Getting enough sleep is important, but it's also vital that you lean into restoration during your resting time. You can't pour from an empty cup, so caring for yourself well means keeping your own cup filled, whether it's making time to exercise each day, reading, listening to music, writing, working in your garden, or even watching your favorite TV shows.

| Which activities are restorative for you?

Do those activities help you connect with God and His love for you? If not, think of activities you can do that will draw you closer to God and to love.

WEEK 10

Rest Is a Gift from God

It's useless to rise early and go to bed late, and work your worried fingers to the bone. Don't you know he enjoys giving rest to those he loves?

PSALM 127:2 THE MESSAGE

Work can feel all-encompassing, especially if you work from home or work a job that you can take home with you. You might be sorting through emails on your phone and a laptop, and even though you're at home, you're not resting. Productivity does not equal health, no matter how much you love what you do. Work guilt is real, and you aren't alone in feeling it.

One essential way to take care of yourself is to press pause on the office (including *thinking* about work) at the end of the day. Rest has become synonymous with weakness in our society, but God has never seen it that way. Rest is a gift on so many levels. Running yourself ragged only leads to burnout, but rest helps you to be more productive and innovative when you are on the clock.

How often do you work outside of normal work hours?

Do you find that it takes you more time to do tasks when you do that? Why or why not?

What could you be doing to rest and restore yourself during that time instead?

WEEK 11

Get Moving

She wraps herself in strength, carries herself with confidence, and works hard, strengthening her arms for the task at hand.

PROVERBS 31:17 THE VOICE

Regular exercise is an excellent way to take care of your body and your mind. It releases *serotonin*, which is a mood-boosting brain chemical that makes you feel happier and more energetic. Let's face it, God didn't stock the Garden of Eden with laptops and ergonomic chairs. We were not created to spend all our time sitting in front of screens. You are created to move and walk and enjoy the magnificent body God designed for you. You don't have to do CrossFit or run a marathon. Just head outside for a stroll through your neighborhood or do fifteen minutes of yoga on your back porch. Getting into nature and exercising feels good, especially if you make it a habit.

What types of exercise are most appealing to you? Why?

Sometimes we all need a little push to get into the exercise habit. Here are a few ideas to get you started, but feel free to add your own at the end. Just remember to be kind to yourself if it takes a while to get going!

- Commit to a class or workout program with a friend you don't want to let down.
- Pick a podcast you love, and only listen while you are walking.
- Reward yourself with your favorite breakfast when you start your day with a workout.
- Join an exercise challenge via social media so friends can cheer you on.
- Ask a buddy to hold you accountable.
- ______________________________

- ______________________________
- ______________________________

WEEK 12

Combat Stress

Tonight I will sleep securely on a bed of peace because I trust You, You alone, O Eternal One, will keep me safe.

PSALM 4:8 THE VOICE

Stress affects your body physically. When you start to stress, adrenaline surges, elevating your heart rate, increasing your blood pressure, and all of that can lead to shakiness, headaches, and brain fog. The best way to combat stress is as simple as breathing.

Take a few minutes when you feel stressed to close your eyes and take deep belly breaths. As you breathe in, imagine that the air you are inhaling is filled with God's peace and love for you. Notice how it fill your lungs and settles into your body. Then breathe out while imagining that you are exhaling your stress and tension. Keep doing this until you feel calmer and more grounded in God's love.

| How did that breathing exercise make you feel?

What else might you picture as you inhale and exhale that speaks more personally to you?

WEEK 13

Choose Wisely

"I have the right to do anything," you say—but not everything is beneficial. "I have the right to do anything"—but not everything is constructive.

1 CORINTHIANS 10:23

Just because you *can* do something—go out for dinner every night, stay up late binge-watching the hottest new show, drink only juice to try to lose weight—does not make it a good idea. A big component of self-care is exercising wisdom when it comes to choosing what your body needs to feel and perform at its very best. Temptation is everywhere, and, in the moment, ice cream for dinner may seem like a great idea, but you know it isn't. Choose what you need to be your healthiest, whole self, not just what you want in the moment.

Which less-than-healthy choices are you most guilty of giving in to?

Which uncomfortable feelings are those urges and cravings related to?

What are healthier choices you can replace them with that will satisfy that same urge in a wiser way?

OFF
ON
ISO
A-DEP
IMAGE STABILIZER
50mm 1:1.8
Nikon
AF-S DX NIKKOR

PSALM 103:9
529
PSALM 101
PROMISED FAITHFULNESS
TO THE LORD
PSALM 103
PRAISE FOR THE LORD'S MERCIES

Spiritual Care

Spend Time with God

Jesus stood and shouted to the crowds, "Anyone who is thirsty may come to me! Anyone who believes in me may come and drink! For the Scriptures declare, 'Rivers of living water will flow from his heart.'"

JOHN 7:37–38 NLT

Time with God is the ultimate form of self-care. He, and He alone, offers the care we all truly need. He is waiting for you, holding out His arms to pull you close and offer you His love and healing. So often, when life gets busy, we push the quiet, contemplative time we need with God to the bottom of the list in favor of cooking, cleaning, work, school, carpool, practices, games, and the other millions of things that have to be done.

Jesus knew how easy this could happen to us. When He stopped in a small village on His way to Jerusalem, He met two very different sisters, Mary and Martha. Martha immediately made herself busy (and frantic) preparing food and drinks for Jesus and His disciples, which was no small feat. Cooking for thirteen hungry men at the last minute? It's no wonder she felt stressed!

Mary usually would have helped her sister with the work, but instead, she was drawn to Jesus. She sat at His feet, enraptured by His teaching. Martha, understandably, was furious. How was she supposed to do all of that cooking alone? She even demanded that Jesus send Mary in to help, but Jesus refused, saying, "Oh Martha, Martha, you are so anxious and concerned about a million details, but really, only one thing matters. Mary has chosen that one thing, and I won't take it away from her" (Luke 10:41–42 The Voice).

Getting stuff done is important, especially when people are counting on you. Martha wasn't wrong to want to care for people coming to her home. After all, someone has to feed everyone, right? But it is important for us to care for ourselves as well, and there is no more important, fulfilling, life-changing form of self-care than drawing close to God and being enraptured by His teachings and His great love for us. We need to be a Martha to get things done, but, in order to care for ourselves, we also need to be a Mary.

WEEK 14

You Are Already Saved

"For God so loved the world that He gave His only begotten Son, that whoever believes in Him should not perish but have everlasting life."

JOHN 3:16 NKJV

Tuck God's truths away in your heart. Holding on to those promises and thinking about them every day is a form of self-care that should not be underestimated. The truth is that God loves you *so* much He sent His only Son to die *for you*. Even when you feel overwhelmed, reminding yourself how deeply and unconditionally you are loved will help. This truth allows you to take a few deep breaths, slow down, and let God's love for you surround you with comfort and peace.

Prioritize quiet time with your Father this week, and explore some of His other promises:

- Joshua 1:9
- Isaiah 26:3
- Philippians 4:7
- John 15:7
- Mark 13:11
- Romans 8:28
- 2 Corinthians 7:6
- Psalm 116:5–6
- James 1:2–3
- Deuteronomy 33:27
- Genesis 15:1
- James 4:8
- Hebrews 13:5

Which of those promises is your favorite? Why?

Which of those promises have you already seen fulfilled in your life?

WEEK 15

Talk to God

Devote yourselves to prayer, being watchful and thankful.

COLOSSIANS 4:2

Maybe you pray when things are tough, and you pray a little less when life feels easy and it's going your way. But your relationship with God will flourish when you talk to Him like a friend. God doesn't just want a laundry list of your accomplishments or failures for the day. He wants to hear how you're feeling, what is worrying you, what you're dreaming about, and any other little thing on your mind. The more you open your heart up to Him, the more you will feel His peace and His presence in your life.

| How often do you talk to God?

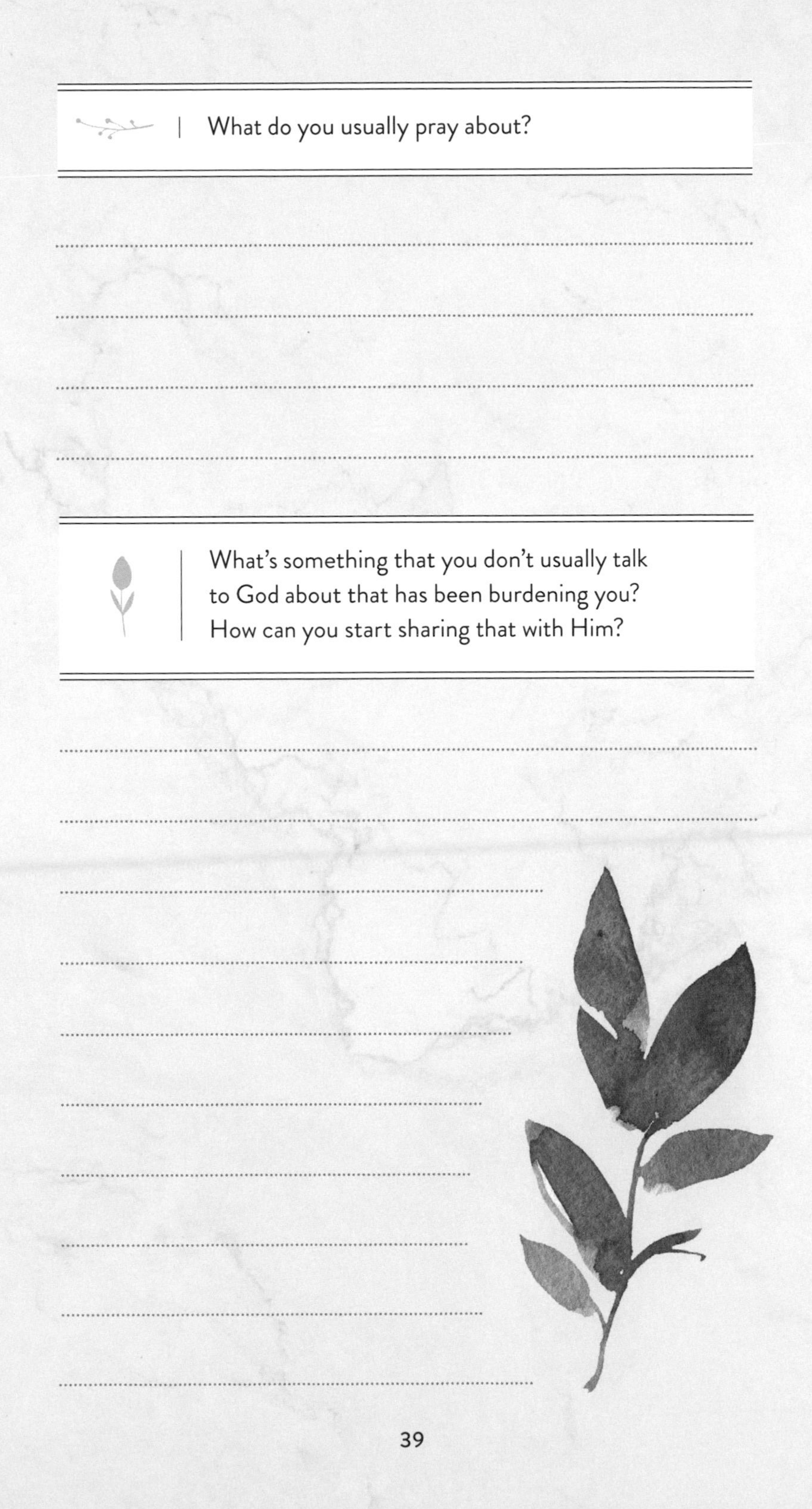

What do you usually pray about?

What's something that you don't usually talk to God about that has been burdening you? How can you start sharing that with Him?

WEEK 16

Listen to God

"The L*ORD will guide you always; he will satisfy your needs in a sun-scorched land and will strengthen your frame. You will be like a well-watered garden, like a spring whose waters never fail."*

ISAIAH 58:11

Prayer is only half of what it means to have a conversation with God. If you spend all of your time talking, you miss out on the things God is trying to tell you or show you in return. Sometimes caring for your spiritual health is about being still and listening for God. He often works in ways that are mysterious, but His ways are not *your* ways. When God "speaks" to you, it may be subtle, like guiding you toward specific people or nudging you to read a verse in the Bible. Listening to God might mean paying attention to the things on the path before you.

The more time you can spend listening to and paying attention to God's presence, the easier it will be to notice those little internal nudges from the Holy Spirit that steer you away from a certain choice or prompt you to go talk to a stranger. Spend quiet time today just breathing and listening for His voice.

Is being still and listening already part of your prayer life? If not, how can you start adding in this practice?

Have you ever heard or felt a reply from God when praying? How did it make you feel?

WEEK 17

God Is Listening

I waited patiently for the LORD; he turned to me and heard my cry.

PSALM 40:1

Sometimes God can feel really far away. You pray and pray, but it feels like God always says no or that He hasn't even heard you. Those times can test your patience, but have faith that God has not abandoned you. He is always listening. He hears each prayer and is always working for your good. There will be times when you can't see what He's doing or how He's already making a way for you. Build up your faith when you feel closest to God so that you have it to fall back on when times are tough and God seems quiet.

Have you ever felt far away from God? Why? What was happening in your life?

What changed that helped you feel more connected?

WEEK 18

Study God's Word

All Scripture is God-breathed and is useful for teaching, rebuking, correcting and training in righteousness, so that the servant of God may be thoroughly equipped for every good work.

2 TIMOTHY 3:16–17

Unplug and focus on God. Switch your phone to silent, close the door, put on some quiet music, and dedicate time to your spiritual health. Get out your Bible and immerse yourself in the beauty and truth of His words, instruction, and promises for you.

The more you study, the more wisdom you will gain, which will allow you to make better, more faith-filled choices for your life and will draw you closer to God.

Which books of the Bible do you feel most drawn to? What do you think God is telling you there?

In what other ways do you see and feel God's presence around you?

WEEK 19

Memorize Verses

Grow in the grace and knowledge of our Lord and Savior Jesus Christ. To him be glory both now and forever! Amen.

2 PETER 3:18

God's Word is a gift when it comes to self-care. His promises, assurances, and words of love and grace are life-giving in so many ways. The verses that are most helpful when you need a boost of love or strength from God are worth memorizing, tucking away in your heart to always have with you. In moments of need, His truth can be a balm of care to your soul. Start with some of your favorites or the verses in this book. Keep track here as you add to your collection.

WEEK 20

Put God's Word into Action

For this very reason, make every effort to supplement your faith with virtue, and virtue with knowledge, and knowledge with self-control, and self-control with steadfastness, and steadfastness with godliness, and godliness with brotherly affection, and brotherly affection with love.

2 PETER 1:5–7 ESV

God doesn't want you just to study His Word—He wants you to *live* His Word. Reaching out and showing love to others can be an unexpected form of self-care. If you're like most people, you often get so caught up in your own worries and problems that it's easy to forget you are part of a much larger community. Going out of your way to help others will remind you of the bigger picture and help put your worries and problems in perspective.

| How can you help someone today?

....

....

....

What organization or cause do you feel called to?

How can you make serving this organization or cause part of your monthly or weekly schedule?

WEEK 21

Use Your Gifts

Use whatever gift you've received for the good of one another so that you can show yourselves to be good stewards of God's grace in all its varieties. If you're called upon to talk, speak as though God put the words in your mouth; if you're called upon to serve others, serve as though you had the strength of God behind you.

1 PETER 4:10–11 THE VOICE

God gave you your passions and gifts and interests for a reason. He wants you to use and delight in them the same way that He delights in them. These are the things you were created to do and use. Think about a time when you were doing something you were incredibly good at. Did you get in the zone and find time falling away as you pursued your work? Those feelings of purpose and joy you have when you are doing the good work you were created for will feed your soul.

| What are your strengths?

What do you feel called to do?

How can that work be used for the good of others?

WEEK 22

Quiet Patience

*My soul quietly waits for the True God alone;
my salvation comes from Him. He alone is
my rock and my deliverance, my citadel
high on the hill; I will not be shaken.*

PSALM 62:1–2 THE VOICE

Sometimes self-care means waiting with quiet patience. When you feel overwhelmed, you, like most people, tend to grasp at straws, looking for anything that might help you. But God doesn't want you to just jump from bubble baths to face masks to yoga. While those things can all be beneficial, they won't fix your problems. God is the only One who can give you true rest and healing. The next time you feel overwhelmed, turn to God first in quiet patience, and see how He guides you toward the best kind of rest.

What are some self-care solutions
you've been jumping to lately?

Have any of those things given you the true, genuine healing you need?

Have you tried giving those problems over to God instead? Why or why not?

WEEK 23

Give It to God

"Are you tired? Worn out? Burned out on religion? Come to me. Get away with me and you'll recover your life. I'll show you how to take a real rest. Walk with me and work with me—watch how I do it. Learn the unforced rhythms of grace. I won't lay anything heavy or ill-fitting on you. Keep company with me and you'll learn to live freely and lightly."

MATTHEW 11:28–30 THE MESSAGE

Sometimes life feels so incredibly heavy. It can feel impossible to follow the unforced rhythms of grace when you are carrying too much. Those are the times when the best thing you can do to care for yourself is to ask for help. Give all of your worries, anxieties, and problems over to God, and let Him carry them and give you rest instead. Nothing is too heavy for Him. He wants to help you, to show you a lighter, freer way to live with Him. Trust and set down your burdens.

Have you truly given your burdens over to God? Or are you still trying to control the outcomes yourself?

How did it feel to pass those problems you were carrying off to God?

WEEK 24

Heed God's Wisdom

One of those days Jesus went out to a mountainside to pray, and spent the night praying to God. When morning came, he called his disciples to him and chose twelve of them, whom he also designated apostles.

LUKE 6:12–13

Following God's guidance is a form of self-care that many people overlook. But His ways are always the best ways, so choosing to follow God's wisdom, even if the path looks more difficult or unclear, is a brave act of submitting to God's care. Jesus knew this. He had many followers early on, too many really. He knew He needed a smaller core group. He could have picked out His favorites from the crowd, but He wanted to hear what His Father had to say. Jesus trusted His Father to care for Him wisely and completely. So Jesus prayed all night long, and then He returned with God's wisdom in hand to choose His twelve disciples.

Where could you use God's wisdom in your life?

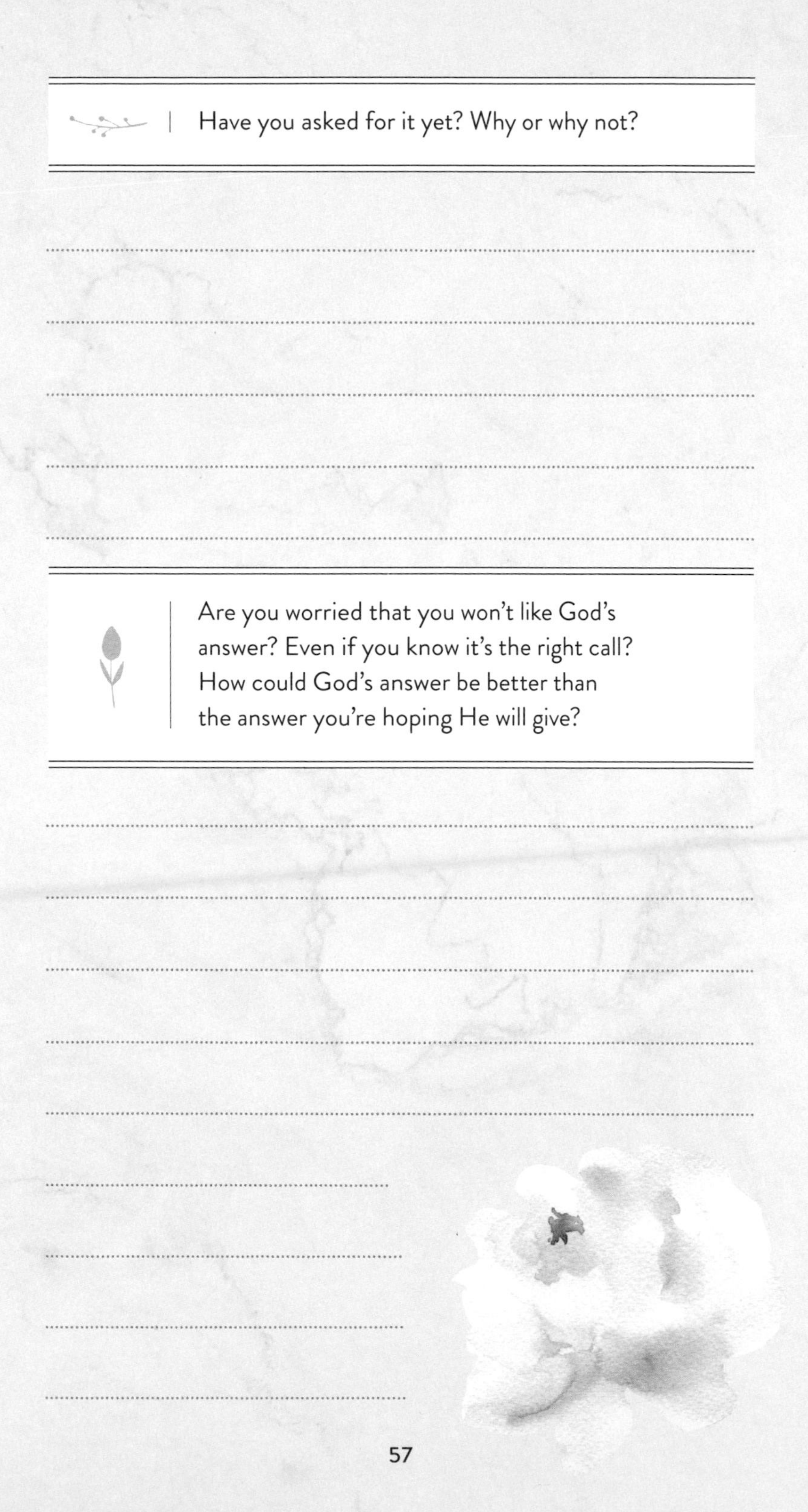

Have you asked for it yet? Why or why not?

Are you worried that you won't like God's answer? Even if you know it's the right call? How could God's answer be better than the answer you're hoping He will give?

WEEK 25

Get Creative

God created man in His own image; in the image of God He created him; male and female He created them.

GENESIS 1:27 NKJV

God created us in His image, and He is the ultimate fount of creativity, which means that we are also driven to create. Making something beautiful from nothing connects you more fully to God. Be it art, pottery, dance, writing, quilting, knitting, woodworking, or any other form of artistic expression, pick something that seems fun to you and let your creativity flow. It doesn't have to be perfect (or even good!). It just has to come from your heart and soul. You'll be surprised at how good it makes you feel.

Start here with some drawing, doodling, or writing. Then move on to any other medium that's calling your name and keep going. You may just make something beautiful.

WEEK 26

Withdraw

Jesus often withdrew to the wilderness for prayer.

LUKE 5:16 NLT

Quiet time for prayer and reflection is a key act of self-care. It can be difficult to even identify your own needs if you are constantly on the go and surrounded by others, and it's even more difficult to hear God when you are living in a constant state of overstimulation or inundation.

Take time to withdraw from the hustle and bustle and go into the wilderness—or at least into the nature in your own backyard or local park. If the weather doesn't allow for outdoorsy activities, find a quiet room with a view you can enjoy while you pray and reflect. Connect with God's creation however you can, and you'll feel closer to Him.

In what other ways or places do you see and feel God's presence around you?

How does the beauty of nature help you see God more clearly?

Date

Date

Emotional Care

Care for Yourself Emotionally

"Peace I leave with you; my peace I give you. I do not give to you as the world gives. Do not let your hearts be troubled and do not be afraid."

JOHN 14:27

Processing emotions in a healthy way is crucial for ongoing self-care. Squashing your feelings down, ignoring them, wallowing in them, or using them to fuel hate or grudges is not healthy. You will deal with dozens of different emotions each day, sometimes even each hour. You can't stop them from coming, so the best way to deal with them is to actually *deal* with them.

Learning to care for yourself emotionally means learning to let yourself feel your emotions fully so you can examine them more closely, follow them back to their root causes, and find what they are trying to tell you. Jesus never shied away from His emotions. We see Him feel anger, disgust, frustration, compassion, surprise, shame, joy, and sorrow in the Bible. What we don't see is Him ignoring those feelings or, on the flip side, blowing them out of proportion. He let Himself experience those feelings, and then He turned to His Father to help move forward. It's a powerful example for each of us.

Our emotions are not truth. They are information—and important information at that—but they are not truth. If something makes you sad or jealous or joyful, you need to know *why*. When you ignore those emotional clues, you miss out on discovering something about yourself that you need to know to stay emotionally healthy.

Sometimes our emotions make perfect sense, but other times our emotions can be tricky. Shame often masquerades as anger or sorrow. Jealousy can be traced back to longing and frustration. And emotions that swing wildly from one extreme to another are often covering a deep hurt that needs to be addressed. The information you glean from your emotions can help you understand yourself better and help you identify and name the things you want most. Don't run from your emotions. Instead, let them lead you toward healing.

WEEK 27

Cultivate Joy

A joy-filled heart is curative balm, but a broken spirit hurts all the way to the bone.

PROVERBS 17:22 THE VOICE

There is joy to be found in every day, no matter how broken you may be feeling. It's there; you just have to let yourself see it and enjoy it—even if it's tiny or fleeting. Write down these joy moments and add to the list every day. When you are feeling down, reread the list, and let it remind you that joy is out there waiting for you. You can do the same with things that give you hope, or times when you feel peaceful, or memories that always cheer you up. These reminder lists are an excellent way to prompt self-care when you really need it.

Use the space to write down a list of things that bring you joy. Add to it as joyful moments pop up in your days. Writing down your joyful moments will not only help you to recognize joy more often but also help you linger in it a little longer when God—the joyful One (Galatians 5:22)—sends it your way.

WEEK 28

Turn Away from Jealousy

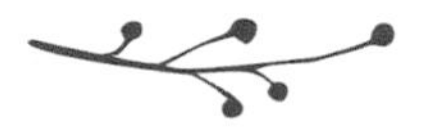

A serene heart can add years to one's life;
but jealous passion rots the bones.

PROVERBS 14:30 THE VOICE

Comparison and jealousy erode any attempts at self-care. They make you feel small and turn your serenity to anger. It is absolutely okay (and smart!) to walk away from anything that is causing a negative response inside of you. And walk away until you get a better handle on it.

Unfollow social media accounts and unsubscribe from email newsletters that send you spiraling into comparison traps. Or, better yet, press pause on social media altogether for a few weeks. If a certain friend brings out your jealous streak, it may be time for a break. This break allows you to let go of those negative feelings and also gives you a chance to better understand *why* you're feeling that way. Use this free time to focus on activities that make you feel cared for and at peace.

Small swaps can make a big difference in avoiding the comparison trap. Instead of mindlessly scrolling Instagram, try journaling about your day. Politely avoid a long conversation with your competitive neighbor in favor of a walk or a bike ride.

Who or what brings out your jealous side or causes you to make comparisons and feel unworthy? How can you politely take a break from those situations?

What are some swaps you can make today?

WEEK 29

Fight Fear

"This is my command—be strong and courageous! Do not be afraid or discouraged. For the LORD your God is with you wherever you go."

JOSHUA 1:9 NLT

Constantly feeling fearful is another emotional state that can really drag you down. It's true that the world can be a frightening place and the future can sometimes seem terribly uncertain, but it's also true that good things happen every day. The best ways to care for your emotional outlook are to focus on the good and limit your exposure to situations that trigger fear.

Stay informed via a daily news recap instead of doomscrolling through headlines all day. Start and end your day by thinking through what you are grateful for instead of letting your worries run away with you. It won't always be possible to avoid the scary stuff in life, but you can keep your eyes set on God and the good He is working in your life when fear strikes.

What are the fears you are battling right now?

What are the good things in your life that you are grateful for?

WEEK 30

Set Boundaries

Better a patient person than a warrior, one with self-control than one who takes a city.

PROVERBS 16:32

Sometimes saying no is an act of self-care. It is important to set boundaries for yourself to protect your emotional health. Respectfully opting out of commitments, responsibilities, and activities that don't align with your personal goals and priorities is the only way you will have the time and energy to say yes to the things that really do matter to you. Having the ability to easily say yes to the things you are excited and passionate about will make any awkwardness at saying no to other things worth it.

Is there something in your life you want to say no to right now? What is it? Do it today!

How did it feel to say no?

Is there something you want to pursue but haven't had time for? What can you say no to in order to free up that time?

WEEK 31

Burnout Is Real

There is hope for a tree that has been cut down; it can come back to life and sprout.

JOB 14:7 GNT

Any one of us can get overwhelmed and feel over it when there is too much pressure for too long. When you are good at what you do, people will ask for more and more until you can barely keep your head above water. At that point, your mind is working overtime, pushing your emotions into overdrive until you shut down. It's called burnout, and it's not a good place to be.

Your mind and emotions need rest as much as your body does. You absolutely need time off the clock to regain your mental and emotional equilibrium at the end of each day. Find hobbies and outlets that inspire your creative side, and give yourself a break from your usual routine. Set boundaries and stick to them to carve out time that is sacred for your care.

Which activities do you find help you turn off your "work" mind at the end of the day?

How often do you make time each week for those activities? What are some adjustments you can make in your schedule to make more time for those activities?

How often each week do you find yourself working overtime, even if it's just running through the next day's to-do list or turning work problems over in your mind?

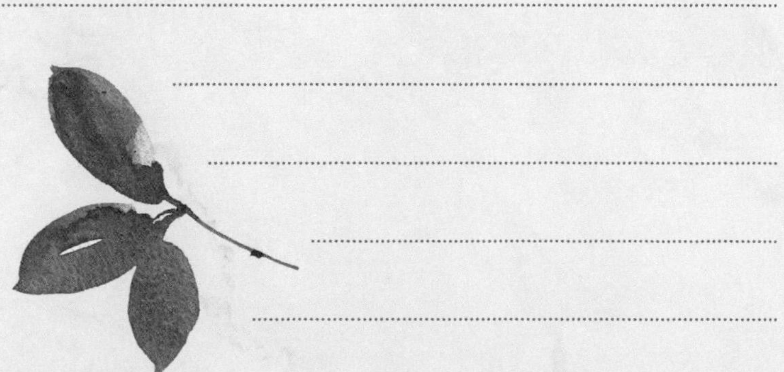

WEEK 32

Forgive

Put on then, as God's chosen ones, holy and beloved, compassionate hearts, kindness, humility, meekness, and patience, bearing with one another and, if one has a complaint against another, forgiving each other; as the Lord has forgiven you, so you also must forgive. And above all these put on love, which binds everything together in perfect harmony.

COLOSSIANS 3:12–14 ESV

Forgiveness is a key tenet of Christianity, but also an important part of self-care. When we hold on to hate and anger, it poisons us from the inside. Working through our emotions, hurt, and anger in healthy ways will naturally lead us to forgiveness. It's something you do as much for yourself as for the person who hurt you. You don't have to receive an apology to forgive someone or even ever tell them that you've forgiven them. And forgiving someone certainly doesn't mean you are giving them *carte blanche* to hurt you again. It means you have processed the hurt you once felt and are ready to let it go, while still maintaining firm boundaries so you can continue to heal.

Is there someone you haven't been able to forgive? Who is that person?

Why do you think that pain and anger is still strong enough to stop you from forgiving them?

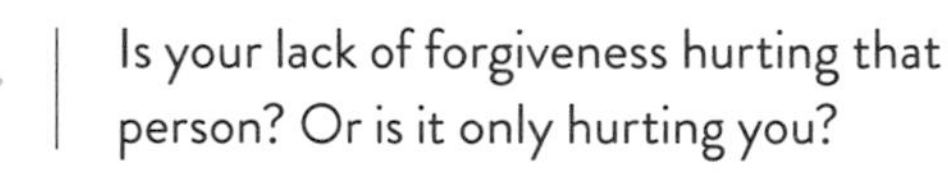

Is your lack of forgiveness hurting that person? Or is it only hurting you?

WEEK 33

Let Love In

"So now I am giving you a new commandment: Love each other. Just as I have loved you, you should love each other. Your love for one another will prove to the world that you are my disciples."

JOHN 13:34–35 NLT

So often we confuse self-care with selfishness, but self-love and self-care aren't selfish at all. Treating yourself with love and tender care allows you to open up more fully to receive the love that Jesus has freely given you. Then you'll be better able to pour that love out to other people. Jesus' deep and abiding love is always available to you, but when you are wrapped up in your own emotional pain and stress, His love can feel totally inaccessible. By making the effort to process your emotions in healthy ways, it will be easier for you to see and feel the love that is always there, waiting to comfort you.

When do you feel Jesus' love most strongly?

When is it most difficult to feel connected to Jesus?

What helps you connect more closely with Jesus when you have been feeling distant from Him?

WEEK 34

Feel Your Feelings

Go ahead and be angry. You do well to be angry—
but don't use your anger as fuel for revenge. And
don't stay angry. Don't go to bed angry. Don't give
the Devil that kind of foothold in your life.

EPHESIANS 4:26–27 THE MESSAGE

It is healthy to let yourself feel your feelings. There are no "wrong" emotions. Your emotions may not make sense to everyone, but they are how *you* feel in that moment. Emotions are information that can help lead us to figure out deeper problems, but we can only receive that information if we let our feelings in and then follow them back to their root cause. Feelings of anger can pop up when you feel out of control or ashamed. Sadness can be masking guilt or longing. Finding the truth that your emotions are pointing to will help you address your true needs.

| What emotions are you feeling in this season?

Why do you think those emotions keep popping up?

Where do you think those emotions are leading?

WEEK 35

Speak Kindly

Kind words are like honey—sweet to the soul and healthy for the body.

PROVERBS 16:24 NLT

You live most of your life inside your head, so do your best to make sure it's a nice place to be. Yours is the voice that you hear most often. What you say to yourself—whether out loud or in your head—directly impacts your emotional health. Choose to speak kind words to yourself. A great way to care for yourself is to start or end your day with uplifting affirmations. Think through what you would love to hear from the people in your life and say those things to yourself. Remind yourself that you are loved, worthy, and valued, just as you are.

What have you been mentally beating yourself up about lately?

How could you speak to yourself more kindly about that situation?

What do you need to hear today? Can you choose to say it to yourself and believe it?

WEEK 36

Resist Temptation

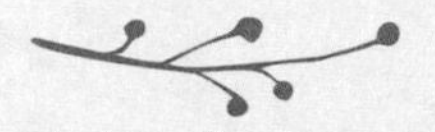

Any temptation you face will be nothing new. But God is faithful, and He will not let you be tempted beyond what you can handle. But He always provides a way of escape so that you will be able to endure and keep moving forward.

1 CORINTHIANS 10:13 THE VOICE

Strong feelings can lead to some serious temptation, especially if you haven't been taking care of yourself emotionally. Ignoring your feelings doesn't actually make them go away, and neither does telling yourself and everyone else that you are fine. Eventually those unresolved feelings will demand to be heard and dealt with, and usually at the worst possible time. You might find yourself reaching for a bottle, or a cake, or calling someone you know is bad for you just to numb the pain when those repressed emotions burst through—and that isn't where you want to be. The best way to avoid temptation (or to have the courage to walk away when temptation is in front of you) is to deal with your emotions as they arise so they don't build up and carry you away.

| What activities help you process your feelings?

Do you have a tendency to ignore or repress your emotions? If so, why?

What temptation.s are you most likely to give into? Why?

WEEK 37

Embrace Comfort

When anxiety overtakes me and worries are many, Your comfort lightens my soul.

PSALM 94:19 THE VOICE

When your emotions go haywire, physical comfort can help soothe them. Curl up under a cozy blanket in your favorite pajamas with a big bowl of mac and cheese and watch old movies. Stretch out in a hammock in your backyard with a good book and a glass of ice-cold lemonade. Hit up a fun happy hour with your best friends and dance your cares away. Whatever comfort looks like for you, lean into it for a dose of self-care that will brighten your spirits and help you regain your emotional equilibrium.

What rituals or activities do you find most comforting?

Are you comforted more by time alone or by time with your people?

Where can you add a little comfort to your regular schedule?

WEEK 38

It's Okay to Cry

Jesus wept.

JOHN 11:35

Weeping offers a cathartic release to your body. Part of allowing yourself to feel your feelings is letting your body experience those feelings too. We all cry, and pretending that you don't cry doesn't do you any favors. Some people think tears are a sign of weakness, but there is nothing weak about dealing with your emotions in healthy ways. In fact, it should be celebrated as a sign of strength and wisdom. Sometimes a good cry is what you need to let go of grief, anger, shame, or embarrassment. Jesus wept openly and without shame, and we would do well to follow His example.

| How do you feel after crying?

What helps you cry when you have emotions you need to work through? A sad movie or book? A poignant song?

Do you feel guilty or ashamed when you need to cry? If you do, why do you think that is?

WEEK 39

God Is Healing You

He heals the brokenhearted and binds up their wounds.

PSALM 147:3 ESV

When our emotions are completely overwhelming, the best thing we can do is ask God for healing. Sometimes no amount of self-care will help because you are dealing with something outside of your control. That's when it's imperative that you ask God to step in and care for you. You can always count on Him to come through to soothe your troubled emotions and give you peace and healing.

Have you had times when you were so overwhelmed and heartbroken that self-care just didn't work? How did God come through to care for you during those times?

What can you do to help yourself trust God's good heart when times are hard?

Mental Care

Keep Your Mind on God

I was pushed back, attacked so that I was about to fall, but the Eternal was there to help me keep my balance. He is my strength, and He is the reason I sing; He has been there to save me in every situation.

PSALM 118:13–14 THE VOICE

Most of the battles we fight aren't physical, but mental. We fight internally to find the right thing to do, we fight our own emotions and temptations, we fight our negative thoughts and tendencies, and sometimes we fight off more serious conditions like depression and anxiety. Here on earth, doctors know a lot more about how to heal our bodies than they do our minds. Luckily, we have God, the ultimate Healer, to step in and help us work on our mental health.

The best thing any of us can do for mental self-care is to fix our minds on God and all of the good work He has done and is doing in our lives. Jesus gives us a perfect example of how to do this. Over and over, He told His followers not to be afraid, not to be anxious or worry, not to judge, to forgive anyone who had wronged them, to give thanks in everything, and, most importantly, to trust Him. It is a remarkably positive way of thinking, and, at the time, it was revolutionary. It still is. Following Jesus' teachings is life-changing for our mental health.

We know there will be suffering and difficulties in our lives—that is a guarantee. Fear, anxiety, judgment, hatred, envy, and mistrust all chip away at our mental health, leaving us drained and unsteady when those difficult times come. But mental self-care through bravery, compassion, empathy, love, gratitude, and trust in God foster a mental attitude of peace, strength, and contentment that is difficult to shake, no matter what life throws at you.

WEEK 40

Make a Choice

Do not allow this world to mold you in its own image. Instead, be transformed from the inside out by renewing your mind. As a result, you will be able to discern what God wills and whatever God finds good, pleasing, and complete.

ROMANS 12:2 THE VOICE

God and our culture are constantly at odds. We have a choice. We can take our cues from society around us, or we can choose to follow God's plan for us. Trying to do both will only result in a raging mental battle. There's not enough self-care in the world that will help when you are constantly at war with your own mind. Choose to follow God's will and purpose for your life and put the battle to rest. When your mind is at peace, you are better able to care for yourself in every way. It won't be a one-time decision, but making this ongoing choice is one of the best ways you can care for yourself and your mental well-being.

When do you feel most pulled between your culture and God?

How do you feel when that happens?
How does it most affect you?

What do you think God is calling you to instead? How does that make you feel?

WEEK 41

Own Your Story

God has not given us a spirit of fear, but of power and of love and of a sound mind.

2 TIMOTHY 1:7 NKJV

Journaling is an excellent way to care for your mental health. Writing out your fears, challenges, emotions, and triumphs will help you process everything you've lived through. It also will give you a record you can return to and see how much you've grown and how abundantly God has blessed you. It may take a little time to feel comfortable and get into the rhythm of writing out your thoughts, but it can be very beneficial, especially during stressful and chaotic times.

Unsure how to get started? Try one of these writing prompts:

- Today I was grateful for . . .
- I felt frustrated today because . . .
- I had a big win today and it felt . . .
- I found joy in my day when . . .
- I took a break from my to-do list and did something just for me. It was . . .
- I cared for myself today by . . .
- Today, I felt God nudging me to . . .
- I was so proud of myself today when I . . .
- God answered my prayer today with . . .
- I ran into an old friend today and it made me feel . . .

- Today was tough. My emotions were all over the place. I felt . . .
- I felt rested and refreshed today and was able to easily care for someone who needed me . . .
- I feel like God is calling me to . . .
- I need to take better care of myself. Here's my plan . . .

WEEK 42

Prioritize You

I can do all things through Christ who strengthens me.

PHILIPPIANS 4:13 NKJV

It is never a waste of time to care for yourself. It might feel like it when you have a to-do list a mile long, but you will pay for it later if you don't take care of yourself now. Taking care of your mental health consistently is the best way to prepare for the tough stuff in life.

Would you rather go into battle feeling strong and prepared, wearing full armor with an arsenal of weapons, or already out of breath and limping, without a sword or shield in sight? Taking care of your body will help you feel strong, taking care of your emotions gives you armor to protect yourself, taking care of your mental health sharpens your mind and gives you the weapons you need, and taking care of yourself spiritually means you walk into battle arm in arm with God. God will be there to help you no matter what, but it's better to be prepared, knowing you are much more likely to emerge unscathed and ready to keep going once the battle is won.

When life gets tough, do you lean into self-care or let it fall to the bottom of your to-do list? What can you do to prioritize self-care?

Does prioritizing self-care during stressful times make a difference in how you are able to handle everything?

WEEK 43

In Front of You

"Give your entire attention to what God is doing right now, and don't get worked up about what may or may not happen tomorrow. God will help you deal with whatever hard things come up when the time comes."

MATTHEW 6:34 THE MESSAGE

Each of us can only do one thing at a time. Trying to multitask zaps your energy and will leave you feeling stretched to the breaking point. Our minds weren't designed to focus on so many disparate things at the same time. Care for your mind by allowing yourself to do what you were made to do: give everything you've got to what is right in front of you in this moment. You will find that you work more efficiently and calmly and produce your best work when you do this. It feels counterintuitive at first—especially since our culture constantly screams that more is better—but doing one task at a time completely is an ongoing act of self-care that will carry you much further than trying to do it all at once ever will.

Do you spend a lot of your time multitasking? Would you say that you're good at it? How does multitasking make you feel?

Does thinking about working on one task (and only one task!) until it's complete feel normal or like a luxury? Why does it feel that way?

Do your best to minimize multitasking this week. How did it feel? Did you get more done than usual or less? Why?

WEEK 44

Beauty and Truth

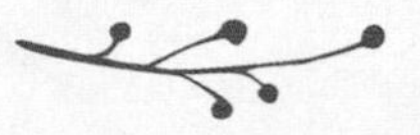

Fill your minds with beauty and truth. Meditate on whatever is honorable, whatever is right, whatever is pure, whatever is lovely, whatever is good, whatever is virtuous and praiseworthy.

PHILIPPIANS 4:8 THE VOICE

Our thoughts are powerful. The things we think about most often and focus on are the things that end up directing our actions. Meditating on worries and anxieties will lead to more fear and more worrying. Meditating on the beauty and truth of God's love and His good work in our lives will lead to a more grateful and loving mindset.

Meditation is the process of clearing your mind, letting yourself be still, and focusing on something in particular, like a specific Bible verse. Psalm 46:10 is a good one. Close your eyes, stay focused on your breathing, and repeat the verse to yourself over and over, letting it sink down into your heart.

As you sit and breathe deeply, your mind will wander. That's okay. Stay aware and redirect your thoughts back to the verse and your breathing as many times as you need to. The goal is not to meditate perfectly but to become more aware of your thoughts so you can focus them more easily on what is good. Try meditating every day this week and see how you feel.

When meditating, what thoughts were most distracting and intrusive?

What verses did you find it easiest to meditate on? Why do you think that is? How did you feel at the end of a session?

WEEK 45

You Control Your Thoughts

The mind governed by the flesh is death, but the mind governed by the Spirit is life and peace.

ROMANS 8:6

A huge part of self-care is learning to control your thoughts instead of letting them control you. This is a tough one! When you focus on things outside of your control, you end up feeling frustrated, helpless, and hopeless. When you focus on what you can control—yourself and your responses—you end up feeling calmer and better able to manage stress. And when you focus your thoughts on God, you are filled with His peace and an abundance of hope and love. It's up to you to choose. Choose care and peace and hope today.

What can't you control in your life right now?

What can you control?

What can you turn over to God's control?

WEEK 46

Lose Yourself in Something You Love

There is a time for everything, and a season for every activity under the heavens.

ECCLESIASTES 3:1

Do you love to read? To hike? To sew or knit? To scrapbook? To bake? Hobbies are an excellent form of self-care, especially when they are things you truly love to do. Of course, life gets busy and you're forced to put those hobbies aside more often than not, but you can get a great mental boost from your hobbies when you set aside time for them. Losing yourself, however briefly, in something that you love doing is powerful and can refresh your mind in surprising ways. Take the time this week to indulge in your favorite hobby and see how it makes you feel.

What are your hobbies?

How often do you make time for them each week? Each month?

Take an hour this week to focus on a favorite hobby. How did you feel when you finished?

WEEK 47

You Aren't Alone

Cast all your anxiety on him because he cares for you.

1 PETER 5:7

You don't walk through this world alone. God is always with you, which means you don't have to carry all of your anxieties and frustrations alone either. You can give them over to God and ask Him to handle them. We forget that, to our detriment. It's good to be able to handle some things yourself, but there is no shame in needing help. You were created with God in the equation, which means that no matter how hard you try, you won't be able to carry it all yourself. You can keep struggling to handle everything yourself, or you can share the load with God and walk more freely and lightly with far more joy.

What can you do to get in the habit of asking God to help you carry your worries and concerns?

When you give your problems to God, do you truly trust Him with them? Or do you keep trying to handle them anyway?

What have you been struggling with that you could give to God today? How would it feel to share the load with Him?

WEEK 48

Count Your Blessings

So then, just as you received Christ Jesus as Lord, continue to live your lives in him, rooted and built up in him, strengthened in the faith as you were taught, and overflowing with thankfulness.

COLOSSIANS 2:6–7

The best way to counter a harried mind is to cultivate a grateful heart. When you live your life steeped in gratitude for all of the things you have and are, the rough stuff doesn't shake you nearly as much. If your mind is grounded in gratefulness, you will be more confident and feel more secure in the hope and faith that comes from that. Start and end each day by counting your blessings. It will be a balm to your heart and mind.

What are the blessings in your life?

WEEK 49

Celebrate

There is nothing better than for people to eat and drink and to see the good in their hard work. These beautiful gifts, I realized, too, come from God's hand.

ECCLESIASTES 2:24 THE VOICE

It isn't self-involved or overly prideful to want to celebrate important moments. In fact, celebration is an undervalued form of self-care. It's actually very beneficial to enjoy the fruits of your labor and to pat yourself on the back for your hard-won accomplishments. No one works hard just for the sake of working, right? We work to get to an end goal, to move forward, to create something out of nothing, to fulfill a purpose. Taking the time to stop, acknowledge, and celebrate when those goals are accomplished, or when you take that next step, will help motivate and inspire you to keep working, to keep leaning into the purpose you've been called to, and to keep finding joy in what you do.

When was the last time you truly celebrated an important moment? How did it make you feel?

What have you accomplished lately that's worth celebrating?

Plan a celebration for it here, and then make it happen!

WEEK 50

Take a Break

The LORD *replied, "My Presence will go with you, and I will give you rest."*

EXODUS 33:14

When your mind starts to feel fuzzy and tired, the best way to care for yourself is to put your work aside for a mental break—even if it's just for a few minutes. If you have the time, take a nap, go for a hike in the fresh air, play a game, do a puzzle, or watch an episode of your favorite TV show. If you don't have much time, watch a silly cat video or go on a short walk around the block. A good rule of thumb is to work for fifty minutes and then take a ten-minute break. But if that's not possible, take breaks whenever you can. You will be able to work more effectively after your mind has been refreshed.

What is your favorite way to take a mental break?

How can you fit more mental breaks into your daily schedule?

Try to take a ten-minute break every hour or two today. How did it feel?

Did taking a ten-minute break make a difference in your productivity? Did it help you feel more rested?

WEEK 51

Be Present

She is clothed with strength and dignity, and she laughs without fear of the future.

PROVERBS 31:25 NLT

It's easy to get so caught up in all the things you still need to do and accomplish that you get ahead of yourself. When you let your thoughts flow forward to your fears for the future, you'll miss what's happening around you right now, and right now is full of good things to be enjoyed and appreciated. Staying present where you are at this moment is a strong form of mental self-care.

Constantly worrying about what's to come will exhaust you mentally, and no amount of planning can truly prepare you for what will happen tomorrow because you aren't in control—but God *always* is. Trust God with tomorrow's problems and let your fear of the future fade away as your mind focuses on today and all that it offers you right now.

What do you most often find yourself worrying about?

What can you control about that? What can't you control about that?

What can God control about that?

What are you missing out on in the present while you are worrying about that?

WEEK 52

Let God Renew Your Strength

Those who hope in the Lord *will renew their strength. They will soar on wings like eagles; they will run and not grow weary, they will walk and not be faint.*

ISAIAH 40:31

When you regularly practice true, meaningful self-care, you will find yourself more aligned with the rhythms of rest and care that God has laid out for you from the beginning of time. You will find yourself leaning into God's love and care for you and living in closer connection with Him. Life lived hand in hand with God is a life steeped in care, both for yourself and for others. It is a life of tenderness, love, peace, healing, rest, and good work. It is the life you were made for, and it's one that you deserve.

Do you feel closer to God when you regularly practice self-care? If so, why?

How has your meaningful self-care changed your perspective on yourself and others?

How has engaging in self-care helped you love and appreciate yourself more?